Bernhard Koch
Believers are winners

BERNHARD KOCH

Believers are Winners!

Going from weakness to strength

ISBN 978-3-96588-004-7

ReformaZion Media
Braasstraße 30
D – 31737 Rinteln
Germany

phone +49 5751 9717 0
fax +49 5751 9717 17
info@reformazion.de
www.reformazion.de

Contents

"Blessed are those men
who hold you as their strength
and follow you from their heart.
They pass through the valley of tears
and make it a place of springs.
And the teachers are adorned with many blessings.
They gain one victory after another,
that one will have to see: the true God be in Zion."

Psalm 84:5-7; Luther Bible 1964

Through these three verses from Psalm 84 I received a deeper understanding of how God will work in us humans while being in the many times desolate valleys of this world. Due to a pleasant urging by the Holy Spirit I want to share this insight. The thoughts of these verses show us a basic principle that we will encounter time and again while reading the Bible.

1

Give me your heart, my son

"Blessed are those men …" Psalm 84:5; Luther Bible 1964

These few words reveal God's attitude toward us. He wants welfare for us!

The word used for "blessed" can also be translated as "happy" – which might be understood easier.

God Almighty desires welfare (or happiness) for humankind. For this reason he repeatedly points out in his word that we can experience his blessing if we will follow his ways.

God wants to give us welfare – both spiritually and materially. To come to know his blessing the psalm tells us:

"Blessed are those men who hold you as their strength …"
Psalm 84:5; Luther Bible 1964

The following translation of this verse is relating to us as well:

"Happy is the man whose strength is in you …"
Psalm 84:5; Elberfelder Bible

If strong in ourselves we cannot walk in the ways of God; self-strength is not helpful to our welfare. The word of God says, we will be happy if we will separate us from obstinacy and do not live by our own strength.

God is strong! His will and strength are predominant. Only he who moves in the will of God will prevail by the power of the Most High.

Every person who loves the Lord and is aware of their own weakness can say: "I am strong in the Lord, strong in the power of his might!" (see Joel 4:10; Ephesians 6:10)

Therefore: Happy is the man who finds his source in Jesus and holds him as his strength – he will experience the blessing of God!

God is not just anybody and not just anyhow – he is exactly as he has revealed himself to the world by Jesus Christ. Jesus is the visible image of the unseen God (see Colossians 1:15; Hebrews 1:3). In the Son of God the Father is showing us what he is like. Those who receive Jesus and adhere to him, their strength is in God.

Jesus tells his followers:

"Anyone who has seen me has seen the Father." John 14:9

We shall not make any image of God – because God has given us his image: Jesus Christ!

There is another important aspect in Psalm 84:5,

Blessed are those men who hold you as their strength and follow you from their heart.

If you want to be able to follow Jesus from your heart, one decision is significant – namely to ask Jesus to be at the center of your heart and to let him rule from there.

No one of us can follow God self-dependently. Only Jesus is able to live according to the heart of God. In our heart he is the force that makes us proper followers. – Hence God calls out:

"My son, give me your heart and let your eyes delight in my ways." Proverbs 23:26

2

Moved by the word

Our heart is the seat of the thoughts. It contains everything that a man has listened to. Jesus says:

"Out of the abundance of the heart the mouth speaks."
Matthew 12:34; Elberfelder Bible

The content of the heart finds its way through the mouth. The words of a man will reveal what is in his heart.

According to the epistle of James our tongue directs the whole person (cf. James 3:1ff.). Every man will move toward the exact place where he is talking himself to. To be able to follow Jesus in the right way, we need to hold fast to him and his words in our hearts. His words spoken by us are leading us his way. – The Son of God says:

"If you remain in me and my words remain in you, ask whatever you wish, and it will be done for you." John 15:7

In other words, this verse says: "If you remain in me and my words abide in you, you will speak my words and thus they will be done for you."

Whoever abides in Jesus and has his word dwelling in his own heart, is guaranteed to follow God in the right way.

Those who speak the words of God with their mouth are led to God. In this context James says:

"Come near to God and he will come near to you." James 4:8

***

"Blessed is the man who does not walk in the counsel of the ungodly, nor walks on the path of sinners ..."

Psalm 1:1; Luther Bible 1964

Also the first psalm begins with the word "blessed". Blessing surrounds those who do not move in the counsel of the wicked. – Who are the wicked?

First of all, are these not those who stand against God and man? They are evil spirits that have separated themselves from God and – according to Paul (cf. Ephesians 2:1-3) – they prepare the ways for the sinners.

These wicked spirits have sown their thoughts into the hearts of these men: a mesh of lies by religions, philosophies, ideologies and the like. Through their mendacious words they cause an advancing of ungodliness which means the person is no longer moved by the word of God. A person under the influence of these lying spirits is called a "sinner". The Greek word for "sin" is "hamartia", stating to be off target. The goal of life is God!

Lest we drift away from God, the writer of the book of Psalms admonishes us to leave the counsel of the wicked and to follow the truth. – Jesus says:

"I am the way and the truth and the life!"   John 14:6

God wants us to walk the path of Jesus and not to enter the way of sinners. The way of sinners matches that of the wicked spirits. The words of the wicked lead to ungodliness, where ultimately there is no well-being.

Only God gives true happiness. If we have the word of Jesus in our heart then the mouth will confess it. This turns our whole person to the right path which is Jesus. The counsel of the Most High is clear; Paul encourages us: "Carry the word of God in your heart and say it with your mouth "(cf. Romans 10:9+10.) The truth spoken takes us into the life of God.

The Spirit of Jesus says:

**Blessed are you
if you hold to me as your strength.
It will be fine with you.
You will be able to live in blessing
by the strength of my word!
My word in your heart,
spoken by your mouth,
will change every circumstance set against you,
toward your well-being!
Become strong in me! I am your strength!
By my word I am working in you
so that you can follow me from your heart!**

3

Enlightened eyes of the heart

Jesus said to the scholars who had studied the scriptures:

"Are you not in error because you do not know the scriptures or the power of God?" Mark 12:24

Only the knowledge of scripture, understood by the Holy Spirit, releases the power of God. If even the academic, who had employed the holy scriptures since childhood, were wrong and did not know the writings – how much more do we need God's help to gain insight into the Bible. Only the spirit of the word can clarify the scriptures. Every human intellectual attempt to fathom God's word will fail. No spirit of this world can lead us into truth. Religious, philosophical and ideological spirits rather have an interest in leading us astray, away from God.

To open the eyes of the church at Ephesus for the depths of the knowledge of Christ, Paul prayed,

"... that the God of our Lord Jesus Christ, the glorious Father, may give you the Spirit of wisdom and revelation, so that you may know him better. I pray that the eyes of your heart may be enlightened in order that you may know the hope to which he has called you, the riches of his glorious inheritance in his holy people, and his incomparably great power for us who believe. That power is the same as the mighty strength he exerted when he raised Christ from the dead and seated him at his right hand in the heavenly realms." Ephesians 1:17-20

We too should ask God in prayer to open our eyes – maybe like this,

"God of my Lord Jesus Christ, father of glory, please give to me the Spirit of wisdom and revelation to know Jesus deeper. Enlighten the eyes of my heart. I want to know what is the hope I am called for by you and what is the richness of glory you have given to me as a saint. Let me comprehend the exceeding greatness of your power for me as a believer. For the power of your strength which you have operated in Christ has started working in me."

When we know the scriptures, the power of God will become apparent in and through us Christians. Letters by themselves are lifeless, but the Holy Spirit makes God's word alive. Only in the living word we will get to know Jesus Christ in his power. The Holy Scripture refers us to Jesus (cf. John 5:39+40). Those who get to know Jesus experience true life. – Knowing Jesus is eternal life (cf. John 17:3).

While Scribes, Pharisees and Sadducees were looking for eternal life in the scriptures they would not come to him who is eternal life. They read the word but could not grasp it. They didn't have any knowledge of Jesus, the living word of God. He who does not see Jesus in the scripture will not experience the power of God. But whoever comes to Jesus has everlasting life and the Holy Spirit will open his eyes to guide him into the truth (cf. John 3:36). And the truth sets us free for the experience of the power of God.

4

The truth sets free

Martin Luther discovered a foundational truth, one that is a prerequisite for the receiving of all biblical promises: God is gracious.

This knowledge – God is wanting to give us salvation without our own merit – released great power for Martin Luther. In the force of this truth he went against the religious leaders, the Roman Church, which at that time no longer taught this truth and pursued other interests. He stood before the emperor and the Roman Catholic Church and preached the gospel. Although he knew this could mean his death, he could not be dissuaded from speaking the truth to those leaders. For such an undertaking a person will need a lot of strength – which Luther received by the truth. In this power and through the belief in the efficacy of the word of God he overcame all fear.

Just like that the word of God wants to lead us into strength. Fear shall be far away from us. – Paul declares:

> **"For the spirit God gave us does not make us timid, but gives us power, love and self-discipline."** 2. Timothy 1:7

Through faith in God's word Luther experienced the spirit of power and not the spirit of fear. Fear is not in love (cf. 1. John 4:18). – John says:

> **"God is love. Whoever lives in love lives in God, and God in them … There is no fear in love. But perfect love drives out fear, because fear has to do with punishment."** 1. John 4:16-18

He who lives in God is in love and has no fear. Because fear is not found in God; rather, fear is an ungodly spirit and therefore sin. The frightened soul has not yet arrived at perfect love.

Martin Luther believed God and followed the command of the Emperor to come to the Diet of Worms. Friends advised him not to go, as repeatedly people who rebelled against the prevailing doctrine of the Roman Catholic Church had been executed.

But the reformer was not deterred. He feared no barren valley. He walked through it making it a place of springs – of which we benefit even to this day.

Luther said: "But even if my foes lit a fire between Wittenberg and Worms that reached to the heavens I will, nevertheless, appear in the name of the Lord and … confess Christ, and let him make of it what he will. Even if there were as many devils in Worms as tiles on the roofs, yet I will go there ..."[1]

Luther did not give any place to fear but boldly went to Worms. But the devil feared such great bravery and tried to stop Luther through disease. The devil trembles because of people who are in Jesus and will not be intimidated. He rightly feared that the truth would be proclaimed by Luther in Worms, reaching the people and opening their eyes.

Despite of being afflicted by disease Luther said: "But Christ is alive, and I will come to Worms, even if all the gates of hell and all evil spirits under the heaven will fight against it."[2]

With that we see, an arid valley actually is a vale of tears for the devil. His defeat is imminent if one will not be fooled and pass through the valley.

Faith in the word of God releases great power and it makes bold. Believing is to say what God says. Whoever agrees with the word of God like that, will act in the power of the Most High.

---

1 H. Korinth: "Dr. Martin Luther: Lebenslauf, Reformation und Augsburgische Konfession", S.5, H. Korinth, Hamburg

2 Marianne Bernhard: "Martin Luther Hausbuch, S. 205, Brief an Spalatin 14.4.1521, Godron Verlag, Bayreuth, 1. Auflage 1983

5

Following Jesus from the heart

"Blessed are those men, who hold you (Jesus) as their strength and follow you from their heart." Psalm 84:5

How can we follow Jesus from the heart? With man this is impossible, but all things are possible with God (cf. Mark 10:27).

Trying to follow Jesus of own endeavor will fail. No one has in himself the required attitude. We need Jesus in our heart to be able to follow him. He and his word must fill our heart. – Jesus says:

"For the mouth speaks what the heart is full of." Matthew 12:34

The mouth reveals what a person has in his heart. The tongue directs the whole person (cf. James 3:1 ff.). Someone who is speaking from a heart filled with the word of God is following the path of Jesus.

In this context I want to come to the speaking in tongues. This is a God-given easement to follow Jesus from the heart.

If our heart belongs to God, our tongue does too! The speaking in tongues is a language that the Holy Spirit gives to our spirit (cf. 1. Corinthians 14:14; Romans 8:26). When we pray in tongues our spirit is praying words inspired by the Holy Spirit.

A ship will be steered with a rudder. Directed by the pilot, it steers the whole ship according to his will. Likewise the Holy Spirit will guide us through our human tongue. The speaking in tongues is therefore of particular importance since the Holy Spirit can lead us by the means of it.

The tongue talker does not understand the words but his inner man will be strengthened (cf. 1. Corinthians 14:4). Every Christian who will be guided by the Holy Spirit and in faith will be speaking in unknown tongues is following Jesus. Also he experiences a faster access to the heart of God. This type of discipleship humbles the mind which many times acts in control, preventing the right pursuit of Jesus. "Trust in the Lord with all your heart and lean not on your own understanding." (Proverbs 3:5)

The Holy Spirit makes us follow Jesus through comprehensible as well as non-comprehensible words. Praying in tongues is the most easy way to be led by the Holy Spirit.

The Holy Spirit guides into all truth (cf. John 16:13) and gives us the essence of the word. He appreciates people who ask for the word of God and want to follow Jesus with his help. By the word and the spirit faith will be generated in our hearts. Faith in action speaks the word of the heart unto salvation (cf. Romans 10:9+10).

6

The heart of God

Christians who are living according to God's heart, previously have received a divine heart. The prophet Ezekiel says that God wants to give us a heart that is well pleasing to him and knows how to follow Jesus in the right way. In Ezekiel 36:26+27 is written:

"I will give you a new heart and put a new spirit in you; I will remove from you your heart of stone and give you a heart of flesh. And I will put my Spirit in you and move you to follow my decrees and be careful to keep my laws."

God created man to be his own image (cf. Genesis 1:27). Therefore the human heart should be conform to the heart of God. But by the separation from God our heart changed: it became stony!

Jesus, the image of the invisible God (cf. Colossians 1:15), again gave us a heart in God's image by his substitutional death on the cross. This is the living heart of flesh. This new heart is in accord with the heart of God. God wants the human heart to contain exactly that what is in his own heart: namely the word of God – which is Jesus (cf. John 1:1; Revelation 19:13).

God's thoughts were shared with us by the prophets. To them God spoke out of the abundance of his heart. Our new heart shall now take up these divine words to get to know the Lord. As we do that by listening we are filling us with the word of God. Our mouth will be speaking out of the full heart and thus directing the whole person into the order of God. Without difficulty soul and body then will be able to live well pleasing to God.

"In the beginning was the word, and the word was with God, and the word was God." John 1:1

Our heart should be filled with what is in the heart of God, which is Jesus, the word of God. When God spoke, Jesus the word became apparent. If our heart is filled with Jesus, we will speak the same way God is speaking. Faith is saying the same as God.

As God said, "Let there be light!" (Genesis 1: 3), the light came forth. Jesus became manifest; he is the light of the world (cf. John 8:12). Today Jesus can shine as the light into the world through us if our heart is filled with him. He says:

"You are the light of the world." Matthew 5:14

Will our mouth be speaking the light of God into the world, then it has become the mouth of God – a prophet. But this is only possible if we were born of God and are in communion with the Holy Spirit who enables the fellowship of the soul with Jesus and the Father.

"Blessed are those men, who hold you as their strength and follow you from their heart." cf. Psalm 84:5

Because Jesus is the word of God in person we can formulate these verses also like this: "Blessed are the people who hold to the word of God as their strength and speak his word by faith!"

The strength of Jesus was his word. Whatever he said happened. And he said,

"I am the truth …" John 14:6

From the truth can only come truth; from the mouth of Jesus therefore came the word of truth.

The truth sets free (cf. John 8:32). It delivers from all bondage resulting from falsehood. The truth is the most powerful person of all. It prevails and its will is unstoppable. Jesus is the truth – which is why his word contains the full power of God. He has been given all power and authority in heaven and on earth (cf. Matthew 28:18). The Lord spoke his word in this power and it happened.

When he said to a sick person, "Be healed!", then it happened by his word. If he ordered demons to leave from people, they had to obey.

Most deeds of Jesus were "word deeds". He was a doer of the word (cf. James 1:22). The might of Jesus came forth through his word.

God carries his word of faith in his own heart – his son Jesus. His word was connected to faith when he spoke, "Let there be light!", and the light was (cf. Genesis 1:3).

The faith of God, which also we are supposed to have (cf. Mark 11:22), comes into our heart by the word of God. If the word is in us, faith comes forth. Faith says the same as God and accomplishes the same works as Jesus did. The Son of God says:

> **"Whoever believes in me will also do the works that I do and will do even greater than these because I am going to the Father."** cf. John 14:12

> **"Everything is possible for one who believes."** Mark 9:23

Just as for God, nothing is impossible to the believer (cf. Matthew 19:26).

He who wants to walk in the power of the word of God and wants to follow God from his heart, just has to confess Jesus as his Lord and let the divine word align himself. The Holy Spirit is leading us into the truth of the word and is helping to understand how it was meant by God. He wants to be our teacher (cf. John 14:26).

He who communes with the Holy Spirit and takes the word of God seriously is living in spirit and in truth (cf. John 4:23+24).

God's spirit enables our heart to carry God's faith in itself. If we are listening to the word of God, he is giving us a heart after God's own heart.

7

A strong heart in dry time

"Blessed are those men who hold you as their strength and follow you from their heart. They pass through the valley of tears (valley of drought, or barren land) and make it a place of springs." cf. Psalm 84:5+6

In our walk with Jesus we will pass through valleys where we will be only in the whining mood. Every human being, whether a Christian or not, must wander through parched, barren valleys. But no one should stay there. The cited psalm specifically speaks of those that are "passing through the valley of tears …"

We must pass through the dry valley. But while there we can change the deserted place into a watery plain.

Unfortunately many Christians when walking in such a valley begin whining. They are getting used to their environment and are stuck. But this lifestyle God has not intended for us.

In verse 6 of Psalm 84 it is not written: when they walk into the valley of tears and stay there, it will become their place of blessing. But it will become a place of springs – as they pass through it.

Those who in this valley give themselves over to the misery are no longer passing through it. Whining holds them there. Only those people will walk through the valley and bring forth blessing that will praise God and move away from the whining.

A drought can have different faces: disease, poverty, suffering by fellow men or demons, war, loss of relatives or friends, lack of peace and joy – anything that will seduce us to wail. Nothing of this God has intended for us.

In such valleys Christians should enforce the will of God and bring about blessing by not looking at the circumstances – but to Jesus. With his word on our lips we can transform every circumstance into a blessing.

Let no one say in such a valley, "I am being tempted by God!" (cf. James 1:13) God does not tempt us to drift from his promise or to start whining.

This valley means challenge and temptation; however this is not caused by God but by the devil. – James writes:

"When tempted, no one should say, 'God is tempting me.' For God cannot be tempted by evil, nor does he tempt anyone … Don't be deceived, my dear brothers and sisters. Every good and perfect gift is from above, coming down from the Father of the heavenly lights, who does not change like shifting shadows." James 1:13.16+17

A valley of tears is not a good gift and not a perfect contribution. The dry valley is being brought about by the enemy and represents an affliction.

By the help of good and perfect gifts from God the arid valleys that we walk through should become places of blessing. – Paul writes:

"And we know that in all things God works for the good of those who love him." Romans 8:28

The valley of the drought is for our good if we make it a fountain. God permits valleys of tears so that we will change them.

As Christians we do not have to accept the will of the devil. The will of God should be made manifest through us – evidently meaning, for us to withstand Satan's will by changing the bad circumstances arranged by him and transforming those into a plain of springs.

The devil hates God and us humans because God created us in his image and by Jesus made us his children. The evil one wants to tempt us to wail and to settle in the dry, desolated valley. He will try anything so we do not enter the promised land.

But God loves us. He has proven his love by sacrificing his Son for us on the cross in order to redeem us from the power of Satan.

Our God who created heavens and earth has not rescued us from Satan's grip by giving material treasures for us. In his eyes we are much more valuable – as precious as he is himself. For this reason he paid for us with the life of his Son. The amount of that price displays we have not been saved solely from the power of darkness, but God also has intended for us to partake in his own nature and his quality of life. Paul notes:

> **"He who did not spare his own Son, but gave him up for us all – how will he not also, along with him, graciously give us all things?"** Romans 8:32

Our Father in heaven wants us to have the same joy for life that he himself cherishes. He does not want to see us stuck in any dry valley but rather to enjoy his fullness. We are supposed to walk in his power and to transform the arid valleys into water springs. To achieve this, in adverse circumstances we have to apply the word of God.

Jesus commands us to pray that his will be done (cf. Matthew 6:10). Not the will of the devil should prevail but the will of God.

God wants us to have the well of life: Christ in us (cf. Colossians 1:27). In him we should refresh us. On the other hand the devil wants to have us whining to keep us away from joy. Because Jesus has our well-being in mind, it says in Psalm 84, Verse 5:

> **"Blessed are those men who hold you** (Jesus) **as their strength…"**

They who look at God himself as their strength and know his good thoughts, know how to move forward in the valley of tears. They will not whine and settle for the drought. Instead, they can rejoice in the valley of tears and leave it behind themselves. James writes:

> **"Consider it pure joy, my brothers and sisters, whenever you face trials of many kinds."** James 1:2

When we are in an arid valley and are being afflicted we have to decide whether we will rejoice or lament.

The Bible urges us to choose joy. Why? Because the joy of the Lord is our strength (cf. Nehemiah 8:10) and we can face the adverse circumstances with boldness. With the help of the Holy Spirit we will bring about change and find blessing. The path is specified in Psalm 84, verse 5:

"Blessed are those men who hold you (Jesus) as their strength and follow you from their heart."

We have learned: only with Jesus and his word in our heart we can follow him wholeheartedly. His word, spoken by us, is the force that directs our whole life into the direction of God.

Through Jesus the Father has given us many promises to rescue us from our troubles. We have to take his promises seriously – for he means what he says. If our heart believes and our mouth proclaims the promises of God, then the Holy Spirit can go to work and change the situation in our favor. The Holy Spirit will bring the truth of the spoken word into visible reality.

The Lord wants us to change the visible by the truth. If the circumstances speak of disease, the word of God will counter: "By his wounds we are healed!" (cf. Isaiah 53:4+5)

We do not have to deny the present situation. But the proclamation of the word of God if believed will bring the truth into visible reality for us, "By Jesus' wounds I am healed!" Let us confess the truth and be set free of any visible disease. – Jesus says:

"If you hold to my teaching, you are really my disciples. Then you will know the truth, and the truth will set you free."

John 8:31+32

The truth sets free! It also delivers from disease. By the working of the Holy Spirit the healing is being made manifest.

The word of God is just as alive as God himself (cf. Hebrews 4:12); and in the power of the Holy Spirit it will bring forth the springs of life. With the word of the Lord we will extinguish all flaming arrows (lies) shot at us by the devil – if we proclaim the word and use it as our shield of faith (cf. Ephesians 6:16).

The devil is a liar! He has come to steal, strangle and murder (cf. John 10:10). All too often we suffer from his lies in our circumstances. Actually he is lying mostly by the circumstances of life.

The word of God in our mouth is the power that changes conditions. The Bible says:

> **"As they pass through the Valley of Baka (valley of tears), they make it a place of springs."** Psalm 84:6

There is no water in the arid valley, it is dry and lifeless. Whether it is a disease, poverty or any suffering, a bad mood or even depression – we should not accept it. With our passage we will make the valley a place of springs or a watered garden. This is our task – not the one of Jesus.

The Son of God has already accomplished everything (cf. John 19:30) and has prepared our action. Through the support of the Holy Spirit we can now speak forth what Jesus has given himself for.

Our mouth is the source of the "water-blessing" for the arid valley. Through the word we transform the dry valley into a well-watered garden. – Jesus says:

> **"Whoever believes in me, as Scripture has said, rivers of living water will flow from within them."** John 7:38

The believer speaks what God says. These words will make streams of living waters flow into the arid valley.

If we counter adverse circumstances with the word of God, it will come into effect and change the situation for the better. Only, we will have to speak it. For this reason we have to know the word of God; only where we have revelation we will have faith – and only faith will lead us to the right confession. The word of God spoken into our circumstances like that, the Bible calls faith applied.

All the time the devil is trying to plant his words of lies into our hearts and elicit a negative belief. This kind of faith the Bible calls unbelief.

In the arid valley Satan wants to give us negative visions and to paint death before our spiritual eyes. For example he will say: "This disease will lead to cancer and end in death. You are a doomed man!"

We must not listen to the devil. He is a liar who seeks to steal from us and wants to take our life.

However, Jesus has come to give us life – life more abundantly.

"I have come that they may have life, and have it to the full (brimming over)." John 10:10

Jesus' words, believed and confessed, will show us visions of the abundance of life. Faith opens to us what the Holy Spirit wants to do, even before it has become a reality in the visible world. The word creates the springs of life in us, even before they are perceived. Those who suffer from sickness should speak the word of God in faith against the disease. They should say: "Jesus suffered for my illness and has taken it upon himself. By his wounds I am healed." (cf. Isaiah 53:4+5)

The truth sets us free from the power of the devil. God's word, used as a shield against the sly attempts of Satan, will negate each of his attacks.

Also I had to learn this lesson. My way led through a valley of misery of disease, in which I found myself for approximately three years. Not that this disease would have tied me to a bed or weakened physically – rather it was psycho terror. The symptoms of inflammation oppressed me, even tough it was not a very severe ailment – when viewed in retrospect.

The voice of the liar spoke to me and tried to persuade me of cancer and death. – I was in God's boot camp. During this challenge I learned to counter the adverse circumstance with the word of God and thereby make Jesus' victory apparent. The word of God spoken from my mouth caused the sickness to eventually have to disappear.

God's word is alive. It is just as alive as he is; it is spirit and life (cf. John 6:63), and in cooperation with the Holy Spirit it discloses the power of God. Spoken from the heart it will accomplish in the visible realm exactly what it says.

Those who have the word of God in their heart, have a strong heart. In difficult times it resists the affliction and through the indwelling power of faith the drought is overcome. Since the mouth speaks out of the abundance of the heart, the barren valley will be transformed into a fertile garden.

8

Looking up to Jesus

While walking through the dry valley a strong heart will transform the drought into a plain of springs. The German Elberfelder translation of the Bible even says in the second part of Psalm 84:6:

"The spring rain covers it with blessings."

A heart strengthened by the word of God is a blessing for the dry valley. Spoken from the heart the word of God is like a spring rain on the valley's dry soil. Martin Luther translated verse 6 differently:

"And the teachers are adorned with many blessings."

Those who teach the word of God should have learned their lesson in the valley of tears. They know how to transform dry seasons into a plain of springs. For this reason they are decorated with a lot of blessings. Their job is to teach what they have learned.

But in the following I want to consider with us the translation of the German Elberfelder Bible. It shows us, we have to water the dry valley with words of blessing – like a spring rain. Thus it is up to us Christians whether the valley of drought remains lifeless or becomes a fertile plain.

We have to confess the word of God against the respective negative circumstances. The spoken word is stronger and of greater effect than temporary and visible realities. We are speaking against the will of Satan as we allow the Holy Spirit to enforce the will of God. We say and shout: "Jesus! Your will shall be done! The will of the devil is not going to come about! Jesus, thy kingdom come and be manifest! Satan's work shall be destroyed!"

The words of the Lord's Prayer, "Thy will be done! Thy kingdom come!", are the basis for our specific prayer in the arid valley to convert it into a plain of springs. If we pray and proclaim like that the blessings of Jesus become visible. God wants the blessing of Jesus to come out of our mouth and to change our situation.

God's word is the blessing of the spring rain. With our mouth we are covering the drought with these blessings. Not Jesus or the Holy Spirit, not even the Heavenly Father will intervene to transform the dry valley into a well. It is our turn; we have to do something. If we will not proclaim the word of God, the dry valley remains unchanged.

The Holy Spirit works with the word of God when spoken by us. Not that he could not act without us – only, does he want that? According to the statements of Psalm 84 he wants to bring about the transformation of the arid valley with and through us. Also other bible passages show us this principle.

Let us hold fast to the confession (cf. Hebrews 2:14) and counter the circumstances with the word of God. While doing this we are supposed to look to Jesus and not to the visible. – Jesus is the author and finisher of faith (cf. Hebrew 12:1+2).

By the word of our faith we are changing the situations and dry valleys of our lives. Jesus is true to his word. If he wants us to proclaim, he will also make sure that the promise will come to pass. Of course, the devil tries to keep his field. He wants to confuse us and bring us to doubt by standing in the way and causing delays.

A doubter should not think to receive anything from the Lord (cf. James 1:5-8) – and in our context: a doubter will not be able to change the drought.

Satan, the adversary, tries to bring us in doubt by telling us lies. He resists us but can not withstand for long if we will defy him.

"Resist the devil and he will flee from you."   James 4:7

The resistance of Satan should not disturb us but rather makes us rejoice. James teaches:

"Consider it pure joy, my brothers and sisters, whenever you face trials of many kinds, because you know that the testing of your faith produces perseverance. Let perseverance finish its work so that you may be mature and complete, not lacking anything."
James 1:2-4

A barren valley represents an affliction. However, the dry valley crosses our way – but does not come from God – to let our faith in the goodness of God waver. In this challenge we are to rejoice and not to whine. Why should joy dominate our life if we do not feel like it? Because we have understood God is true to his word and will free us from the lack. By faith we know exactly the predicament will soon be changed into blessing. James says:

"Therewith … not lacking anything."

Long ago God already has seen the deficiency. We consider the affliction as a sign that he will bless us beyond previous boundaries. Expectantly and joyfully we declare his truth in our situation.

A valley of tears stimulates us to seek God for new revelation.

"For only contestation teaches to attend to his word."
Isaiah 28:19; older Luther translation

The objection should awaken us and get us to align ourselves with the word of God again. The contestation is not worked by God but a temptation by the devil who wants to move us away from the word of God. However, Jesus uses the contestation to lead us to his word and into a deeper understanding of his person.

Unfortunately we too quickly tend to be content with what we already have experienced. But there is more with Jesus – he gave himself for us and with that he gave us all the fullness of God (cf. Colossians 2:8-10), from which we can take now.

The Father, Jesus and the Holy Spirit hate false frugality. One of the names of God is "El Shaddai" – which means the "All-Sufficient" or "All-Bountiful", the One who is free from lack. He, that is more than enough, wants also us to be equipped with abundance. Jesus says:

"I came that they may have life and have it abundantly."

John 10:10; English Standard Version

Deficiency is a pity state! It is an affliction that should open our eyes for us to know: there is more and we should get into the abundance of Jesus.

The church in Laodicea is a picture for the self-sufficiency of many Christians. That is why the Lord spoke to this church and therefore also to many of us today:

"You say, 'I am rich; I have acquired wealth and do not need a thing.' But you do not realize that you are wretched, pitiful, poor, blind and naked." Revelation 3:17

The acquaintance of the valley of tears will let us see our poverty. It shows us our true condition. The dry valley has to do with ourselves. It is a reflection of the constitution of our soul. A droughty soul feels like whining. It is in need of the refreshing water of the spirit. It needs the word of God.

It is necessary that we become aware of the wretchedness of our soul so that we will recognize the urgency to change its state with the help of God.

As the Lord counseled the Christians in Laodicea he also advises us to buy from him gold refined in the fire (cf. Revelation 3:18). This gold is the word of faith. It changes the needy state of the soul and the body. Desolate circumstances become fertile plains. The word of God transforms misery into joy, poverty into wealth, blindness into eyesight, and nakedness is being clothed.

By living waters flowing from us the dry valley shall become a plain of blessing (cf. John 7:38). This is done by us speaking the word of God while walking through the valley. In other words, we are then looking up to Jesus and confessing his word. Jesus is the beginner and accomplisher of the faith (cf. Hebrew 12:2). He begins faith in us and his word spoken by our mouth completes the faith. Any contestation by the devil can be negated this way.

A time of hardship basically shows: Jesus wants to bless us and reveal his gifts for us. The enemy is trying to prevent this.

Once we have crossed the valley of affliction and left deficiency by confessing the word of God, we have become stronger than ever before.

During my three-year long affliction of disease the devil whispered to me unbelief, saying, "this disease will become cancer. God does not want you to be healthy. Soon you are finished…!"

With this lie he wanted to rob from me, strangle and ultimately kill me. And he would have succeeded if I would have budged to his suggestion. But I listened to the word of God. I wanted to know what Jesus was saying about my situation. Therefore I sought after God's word in the affliction and built on it. I looked to Jesus. The hard time of contestation has brought me deeper into the word of God and taught me to attend to it. The faith of God came into my life.

During this time I was also visiting a medical doctor. Doctors only have limited possibilities but are set by God to assist the process of recovery. However, the doctor could not help me.

Thus, I had to base my trust on the word of God. That made me strong against the affliction. I learned to speak the word of God against the disease and realized in Jesus Christ there is a "Yes" to all promises of God. Hence God the Father had said "Yes" to my health.

"For the Son of God, Jesus Christ, who was preached among you by us … was not "Yes" and "No", but in him it has always been "Yes". For no matter how many promises God has made, they are "Yes" in Christ. And so through him the "Amen" is spoken by us to the glory of God." 2. Corinthians 1:19+20

Through Jesus, the father has a "Yes" for every human and therefore a "Yes" for their healing. – Health is the will of God for us.

I realized this "Yes" applies to me as well. God wants all people to come to a knowledge of the truth (cf. 1. Timothy 2:4); because the truth sets us free (cf. John 8:31+32), also of disease.

This insight was very important to me because the devil tempted me, saying: "This time the help of God will not come. Look, your illness already lasts for so long. God has decided you have come to your end."

If it was the will of God that not all, but only almost all people should be of good health, I always would have seen myself among those who will remain ill – or even should die. But since I realized that God has given healing for everyone, it was easy for me to receive this healing through faith in him.

Yet another question was answered. Until then I did not have any insight as to when Jesus wanted to make visible the healing that he had given to me. Because the healing did not become visible right away, I thought, God only wanted to manifest it after a week or a month or maybe even much later. I kept searching for an answer in the Scriptures and found it in the same epistle:

"In the time of my favor I heard you, and in the day of salvation I helped you. I tell you, now is the time of God's favor, now is the day of salvation." 2. Corinthians 6:2

I realized, today is the day of salvation. Now is the time of my healing. Not only in one week's time, or after one month or after one year. In God there is only a today, a now. Jesus wants to bless us immediately, not only tomorrow.

Now God's thoughts and his will for my situation had become clear to me. To each of God's pledges in Jesus there is a "Yes". This "Yes" shall make manifest his promise today and bring healing to people.

Despite of this insight and my prayer healing still did not become manifest right away. – There was yet another lesson to be learned. In the affliction I continued to look to Jesus and I was given the understanding which step I had to go.

This understanding Jesus gave to his disciples by the parable of a widow who would not accept refusal by an unjust judge. Repeatedly she called for her right, which because of her brazen insistence eventually the judge gave to her.

Jesus taught how like the widow we should approach our Heavenly Father, the righteous judge, for our right. The Lord inquired from his disciples:

"And will not God bring about justice for his chosen ones, who cry out to him day and night? Will he keep putting them off?"

Whereupon Jesus provided the answer promptly:

"I tell you, he will see that they get justice, and quickly."

Luke 18:7+8

This instruction I followed and cried out to God my father to give me justice against the powers of darkness who wanted to prevent the healing that was bestowed upon me by Jesus.

Not that by myself I would even own any right before God, but the privilege imparted to me by grace I did not want to be taken from me. My right to health is rooted in Jesus who took upon himself my illnesses (cf. Isaiah 53:4+5). Therefore my health is accessible for me without own merit.

I cried out to God: "My Father, just judge, I come to you by the grace which was given to me by Jesus Christ. Please administer justice for me against the powers of disease that do not want to accept what Jesus has accomplished for me! Through Jesus I have a right to health! And according to his word, today is the day of salvation! Serve me justice, in doing so you will serve justice to Jesus. He has suffered and taken my disease upon himself! My health is his merit. It is the wages of Jesus if by the wounds inflicted on him my healing is coming forth. Give wage to Jesus and healing to me!"

The righteous judge did not take long and administered justice to me. After a short time all symptoms of inflammation were gone. My health was restored.

Even if we have to walk through the desolate valley of tears, God is present and ready to bless us. King David also knew thereof and wrote in such a dry time:

"Even though I walk through the darkest valley, I will fear no evil, for you are with me; your rod and your staff, they comfort me." Psalm 23:4

The Lord is here. He is also with us in the dark valley, prepared to console us. He is only waiting that we will take his word for serious and speak it in faith. By his word in our mouth he wants to make the dry valley a plain of springs.

The valley of tears is an impugnment, a temptation that comes from the devil. In this contestation we should withstand.

"Resist the devil, and he will flee from you." James 4:7

We fight against Satan (cf. Ephesians 6:12; 1. Timothy 6:12) and hold resistance against his circumstances and his thoughts of lies and everything that is coming from him. The disbelief of the devil we oppose by faith. Words and thoughts that are contrary to God's word we always counter with the word of God, confessing it with our mouth.

You can be blessed in the valley of tears by the use of the word of God and watch how the plain of springs comes forth.

"… And let us run with perseverance the race marked out for us, fixing our eyes on Jesus, the pioneer and perfecter of faith …" Hebrews 12:1b+2a

9

From strength to strength

In Psalm 84:7 it is written:

"They go from strength to strength."

It is those people who walk through the dry valley and make it a plain of springs that are going from strength to strength. They cover the dry land with the blessing of the early rain and do not resign in hardship. They bring blessing by speaking the word of God into the circumstances.

Such a Christian changes situations through the power of the word of God. Through his commitment he masters the resistance of Satan and becomes an overcomer.

"Blessed is the one who perseveres under trial because, having stood the test, that person will receive the crown of life …"

James 1:12

The overcomer walks in the all-conquering power of Jesus and reveals the might of God. If we are one with Jesus, we are more than conquerors and go from strength to strength.

"They gain one victory after another."

Psalm 84:7; Luther Bible 1964

We are victorious if we make the dry valley a plain of gushing life – unveiling the life of God by our faith and proclamation. The plain of springs is the site of new power for us.

The whole world lies in wickedness (cf. 1. John 5:19) and is one valley of tears. But by confession of the word we can make manifest the victory of Jesus and unveil springs of living water.

The Christians themselves are those springs of living water. Jesus told the Samaritan woman at Jacob's well:

"… But whoever drinks the water I give them will never thirst. Indeed, the water I give them will become in them a spring of water welling up to eternal life." John 4:14

The water that Jesus offers is his word. It becomes a fountain in our heart once we are drinking of it. This fountain will again release the word; and our mouth is the opening of this well through which God's kingdom shall become apparent.

The enemy wants to prevent the kingdom of God and tries to resist us. But in affliction we shall overcome by the word of God, going from one strength to another and proving ourselves as strong.

Whoever confesses the word of God in miserable situations and does not dissuade from it, resists the devil who then will have to flee. The dreary circumstances change into heights of joy. If this is experienced greater trust in God is gained. Faith grows, and we will walk from strength to strength and from faith to faith (cf. Romans 1:17).

By faith we are changing circumstances. Trials must come as they reveal our lack – which is to be remedied. Although drought periods do not come from God, they help us to get clothed with the power of Jesus.

10

Appearing before God in Zion

Taking the way of Jesus we overcome affliction and change arid valleys into plains of springs. From strength to strength we are walking focused toward God.

"... each appears before God in Zion."   Psalm 84:7

Martin Luther translated the same verse as:

"They gain one victory after another, that one will have to see: the true God be in Zion."

By listening to the word of God we will get to know it. Then we can believe and confess it with our mouth. We will change the circumstances according to the word and manifest the blessings of God. Thus the power of God is coming forth into the visible world and the governance of Zion can be noticed.

Who speaks the word of God confesses that the God of Zion is the true God. Zion is the meeting place of the people of God, from where the government – the rule of God – goes forth.

Christians who by the word have overcome their bleak situation on the one hand appear before God in Zion (cf. Psalm 84:7) and on the other hand make evident that Jesus is the true God reigning from Zion (cf. Psalm 84:7; Luther Bible). Both translations point to the same content, only they show different perspectives.

Christians should demonstrate in the world who truly is God. The world needs to come to know that Jesus is alive. Jesus is the way to the Father (cf. John 14:6) who is the true God in Zion. Exactly in that place we shall appear as well so that the world will recognize on us where the true God is to be found.

11

The early rain of the word

Only a person with Jesus in the heart can follow the Lord from their heart. Jesus is the word of God. We are to draw from the abundance of his word; if then encountering arid valleys we will have the words available which transform dry places into spring plains.

Being filled with the words of Jesus and abiding in fellowship with the Holy Spirit we will have strength and power to transform every negative circumstance into a blessing of God. The true God in Zion will become visible through our actions. The blessings of Jesus, spoken through his word, will cover the dry valley with spring rain. The infinite riches of the glory and power of Jesus are being revealed. This encourages us to move on; the next barren valley will not take a long time in coming. But we will pass through and go from strength to strength, from victory to victory – by confessing the word of God.

In the heart we believe God's word and are justified. With the mouth we confess the word of God and are being saved from the arid land (cf. Romans 10:9+10).

No matter what may come: With his word Jesus has given us a suitable response. Only we have to know this counter-argument, namely his promise:

"The people that know their God will prove strong and take action." cf. Daniel 11:32

We need the strength Daniel spoke of. This we will receive with growing knowledge of Christ. Additionally we need an understanding of the actions of God so that in trials caused by Satan we can behave according to Jesus.

Many years ago with my family I traveled to the French island Corsica. Before we left I was given the same negative prophecy by two different people at different occasions. I was told: "Bernhard, I saw how you will not come back alive. Better stay home!"

I stood against these prophetic words and resisted the trial by the word of God. I knew, God did not want my death. Therefore this had to be an attempt by the enemy to intimidate me. Because I do not listen to Satan I went on holiday to Corsica with my family.

Also I did not give any room to fear. For God has not given to me a spirit of fear, but of power and love and of a sound mind (cf. 2. Timothy 1:7).

In the biblical account of the affliction Job had to undergo the following statement has been related to us:

> **"What I feared has come upon me; what I dreaded has happened to me."**
> Job 3:25

I did not give myself over to anxiety – otherwise the devil could have done to me according to his will. I believed God whose will for me is to live. He says:

> **"The righteous will live by faith."**
> Romans 1:17

I believed the promise of God and therefore I proclaimed his word. I kept saying, especially from Psalm 118:

> **"'The Lord's right hand is lifted high; the Lord's right hand has done mighty things!' I will not die but live, and will proclaim what the Lord has done. The Lord has chastened me severely, but he has not given me over to death."**
> Psalm 118:16-18

These words I kept not only in my heart, but formulated them against the lie of the devil. Particularly the statement, "I will not die but live, and will proclaim what the Lord has done!", I repeatedly kept holding against the evil one.

The whole word of God contains life. God does not want the death of sinners. He wants for them to live. That's why he let his son die in our stead. On this foundation we may receive the goodness of God for us. His prophetic words over us have no negative aftertaste. God speaks to us warmly. For example he will say:

"Do not be afraid!"   cf. John 6:20; Jeremiah 1:8

"I have chosen you and have not rejected you."   Isaiah 41:9

"Do not fear, for I have redeemed you."   Isaiah 43:1

"Whoever comes to me I will never drive away."   John 6:37

"Do not be afraid, for I am with you; I will bless you."

Genesis 26:24

"Do not be afraid … I am your shield, your very great reward."   Genesis 15:1

"For I am with you and will rescue you."   Jeremiah 1:19

Let us be aware: In Jesus we do have a God who not only does good, but also is good (cf. Matthew 19:17). God is not only loving, but he is the love (cf. 1. John 4:16). He does not only give grace, he is the source of grace (cf. Psalm 145:8).

With the help of the kind words of God I saw through Satan's plan who wanted to kill me. Thus in this "dark valley" I sided with Jesus who led me through it safely. At every occasion when the devil addressed me I proclaimed God's word against the statements that should frighten me.

Even during the return trip Satan tried to dissuade me from my confidence by a conversation I followed. On the ferry a woman said to her companion while looking at me: "The journey is not over yet, still a lot can happen." Immediately I resisted the talk of Satan and spoke with a quiet, but firm voice: "I shall not die, but live, and declare the works of the Lord. Neither to me nor my family and not even to the car anything shall occur."

Without any incident we came home unscathed – and with that through this valley. Still on the way home we visited friends in Lörrach,

Germany, who had invited a prophet. We met, came along well and felt led to invite this brother to our church in Rinteln. Together we had wonderful times in the 1990s and annually held prophetic and apostolic conferences. He fitted exactly into what God intended to do with us. – If we would have shied away from our trip to Corsica we would not have met him – at least not at this God-appointed time. It is important to pass through the barren and dark valleys of life as on the other side divine blessings are waiting for us.

The believers in Jesus, who had given the "negative prophecy" I did not condemn. They only had good intentions. However, I gave them to consider: God does not want our death, therefore such prophecies are not deriving from him. Hence words like that come from the devil. God indeed permits these to be spoken so that we will be informed what the evil one has planned and be warned. What we have to do is to resist the adversary and his lies by setting the word of God against him in prayer and proclamation.

By the spirit of understanding everyone of us has to depart from the doings of the evil one. If we lift our voice for understanding (cf. Proverbs 2:3), this godly spirit will help us to distinguish what is from Jesus and what not.

Satan could not accomplish his work. If I had given myself over to the negative comments, I would have gone on vacation either with fear or not at all. I resisted and fought the good fight of faith (cf. 1. Timothy 6:12) and would not be ruled by fear. This victory was mine:

"They gain one victory after another."   Psalm 84:7; Luther Bible

Christians who confess the word of God follow the Lord from their heart. Their mouth speaks out of the abundance of heart and transforms arid valleys into spring plains. They gain one victory after another, so that the true God will be seen in Zion.

The negative prophecies about my life effectuated that I gained strength by the proclamation of the word of God. The Lord does not permit temptations which we could not overcome (cf. 1. Corinthians 10:13). For future temptations the Lord tells us: "In me you are stronger.

By me you have the power to overcome the challenge and bring about victory." – As Paul also we may say:

"I can do all things through Christ who strengthens me."
Philippians 4:13; Luther Bible

We are strong if we withstand in negative circumstances. Our purpose is obvious: We want to appear before God in Zion. Everyone shall see on us, the true God is to be found there.

We will not be irritated. We listen to the word of God, believe it in our heart and confess it with the mouth, so that it will be done and the valley be made fertile.

In the epistle to the Hebrews we are told:

"We must pay the most careful attention, therefore, to what we have heard, so that we do not drift away." Hebrews 2:1

Zion is the mountain of the rule of God and a picture for the Lordship of Jesus that will go forth from Jerusalem. Jerusalem again is a picture for the human heart. Whoever follows Jesus from the heart, speaks the word of God and reveals the reign of Christ.

The world shall see that Jesus is Lord. His reign begins with our proclamation. By the confession of the word it becomes manifest that the true God is in Zion. That is why we pray:

"Your kingdom come, your will be done …" Matthew 6:10

It is easy. The will of Jesus shall be done! He shall prevail, and not Satan. By praying like that we allow the Holy Spirit to reveal God's kingdom in and through us. The kingdom of God shall come and the working of Satan has to pass. Not the will of some sickening spirit shall be done – for God wants our health.

Paul writes: God wants „all people to be saved and to come to a knowledge of the truth." (1. Timothy 2:4) The truth in regard to disease is: Healed by the wounds of Jesus (cf. Isaiah 53:4+5). The truth sets us free (cf. John 8:32). It also sets free from any disease.

God wants us to prosper both spiritually and materially – and for us to be happy. We shall be wealthy and not living in poverty.

The devil on the other hand wants to see us in poverty, sickness and distress, and (if possible) kill us. The will of God however is indisputable. He wants his riches, health and even eternal life to manifest with us.

Jesus bore the curse of the law on the cross and thus has taken upon himself the consequence of our failure. On the cross God's Son became a curse so that the blessing of Abraham could come to us. By faith we have received from Jesus the promise of the Holy Spirit who is here to help us obtaining the entire blessing of Abraham (cf. Galatians 3:9-18).

From Abraham it is reported that he was very blessed. It was his faith in the promises of God that brought this blessing upon him. Also we are set to receive the same blessing from Jesus. By speaking the word of God and proclaiming his promises with thanksgiving we will experience this blessing in our lives.

If we know that God's will is good in any case, then we will speak from our heart: "Jesus! Your will be done!" By this we permit the Holy Spirit to bring about the will of Jesus in and through our lives.

Those who have recognized that God is love want to see his kingdom of love come and will pray: "Jesus! Your kingdom come!" God is love. In him there is nothing evil, because love can not be wicked. Also, evil can not be good, even if many times it appears to be so. God is not a mixture of good and evil. God is good only.

The good God who revealed himself through Jesus wants us to do well just as he does. – Jesus said:

"Ask and you will receive, and your joy will be complete."
John 16:24

Our joy will be complete if we draw from Jesus in faith by speaking his word with our mouth. This is the way the Holy Spirit makes the promises visible. At the same time the glory of God will be seen on our face because we are filled with joy about the working of the Holy Spirit.

That is how it is being revealed that the true God is in Zion. We appear before him in his glory and with that have arrived in our destiny. – Let us take serious the admonition of Paul in order to not miss this goal:

"See to it that no one takes you captive through hollow and deceptive philosophy, which depends on human tradition and the elemental spiritual forces of this world rather than on Christ. For in Christ all the fullness of the Deity lives in bodily form, and in Christ you have been brought to fullness. He is the head over every power and authority." Colossians 2.8-10

Those who receive Jesus in their heart attain the fullness of God with him. They can follow him from their heart and will draw from his wealth.

In our Lord are infinite and incalculable energies. By his word he created the heavens and the earth (cf. Genesis 1:1) and hence the sun and everything else. What is the energy of the sun? And how many suns may there be in the universe that he called into existence?

All this shows his power. Yet he did not lose any of his power or wealth. Jesus, in whom abides the infinite power of his father, is living in us since we have asked him to come into our life.

Now we can take from him. He in us is greater and stronger than all worlds created by him. Hence he is also stronger than the one who is in the world (cf. 1. John 4:4).

In Jesus we are just as strong as he is. In him we have access to the infinite power of God.

We release his power by taking in and believing his word. The believer speaks, takes of the treasures of God into his heart and reveals the true God in Zion: Jesus in us, the hope of glory (cf. Colossians 1:27).

In Jesus we already have been given everything that pertains to life and godliness (cf. 2. Peter 1:3+4). Now it is up to us to draw from this wealth.

***

"Blessed are those men,

who hold you as their strength

and follow you from their heart.

They pass through the valley of tears

and make it a place of springs.

And the teachers are adorned with many blessings.

They gain one victory after another,

that one will have to see: the true God be in Zion.

Psalm 84:5-7; Luther Bible 1964

Appendix

The valley of dry bones

"The hand of the Lord was on me, and he brought me out by the Spirit of the Lord and set me in the middle of a valley; it was full of bones. He led me back and forth among them, and I saw a great many bones on the floor of the valley, bones that were very dry. He asked me, "Son of man, can these bones live?" I said, "Sovereign Lord, you alone know." Then he said to me, "Prophesy to these bones and say to them, 'Dry bones, hear the word of the Lord! This is what the Sovereign Lord says to these bones: I will make breath enter you, and you will come to life. I will attach tendons to you and make flesh come upon you and cover you with skin; I will put breath in you, and you will come to life. Then you will know that I am the Lord.'" So I prophesied as I was commanded. And as I was prophesying, there was a noise, a rattling sound, and the bones came together, bone to bone. I looked, and tendons and flesh appeared on them and skin covered them, but there was no breath in them. Then he said to me, "Prophesy to the breath; prophesy, son of man, and say to it, 'This is what the Sovereign Lord says: Come, breath, from the four winds and breathe into these slain, that they may live.'" So I prophesied as he commanded me, and breath entered them; they came to life and stood up on their feet – a vast army. Then he said to me: "Son of man, these bones are the people of Israel. They say, 'Our bones are dried up and our hope is gone; we are cut off.' Therefore prophesy and say to them: 'This is what the Sovereign Lord says: My people, I am going to open your graves and bring you up from them; I will bring you back to the land of Israel. Then you, my people, will know that I am the Lord, when I open your graves and bring you up from them. I will put my Spirit in you and you will live, and I will settle you in your own land. Then you will know that I the Lord have spoken, and I have done it, declares the Lord.'"

Ezekiel 37:1-14

The people of Israel are in the arid valley of this world. They are dry and have no spiritual life from God in themselves. This state shall not remain unchanged. Even before Christ the prophet Ezekiel foresaw that this people would be gathered in their own country again and be brought back to life.

By the prophetic word the Lord will collect the people of Israel, spiritually parched in the world, and bring them again into the land of their fathers. He fetches them out of the valley of tears, the valley of dry bones, giving them new life. Ezekiel shows, the Lord applies the principles of faith from Psalm 84:5-7 to make this happen.

Ezekiel was brought to the valley of tears and there he should prophesy over the bones of the dead, so that they would be joined back together. Ezekiel did what the Lord told him.

After the bones of the dead were restored again but still had no life in themselves, the Lord told Ezekiel to invoke the Holy Spirit. Also in this Ezekiel was obedient and said to the Holy Spirit: "Come, breath, from the four winds and breathe into these slain, that they may live." Hereupon the Spirit of God came and by his breath gave life into the dead, so that they were made alive again.

The valley of tears, the valley of the dead, became the valley of life. Through the mouth of the prophet, the Holy Spirit began to work and acted according to the word of God. In new life the awakened bones appeared before the true God in Zion.

Bernhard Koch

The Mystery of the Maharishi of Mt Kailash

Sadhu Sundar Singh meets the over 300-year-old prayer warrior of Christ

In the beginning of the last century the Indian Christian Sadhu Sundar Singh met a very old prayer warrior on the roof of the world – the Maharishi of Mt Kailash.

Called by Jesus the Maharishi has been interceding for the church of Christ since many years. In the process he has remarkable experiences with the spiritual realm, which are almost unknown to people from the western world. The story of the Maharishi is nearly unbelievable. It reaches far beyond our previous comprehension of what one can experience with heaven now.

Sadhu Sundar Singh has been called the "Apostle of India". He has preached the message of Jesus Christ in many villages and towns of his home country, but also to surrounding nations. His proclamation and exemplary conduct of life fascinate his fellow countrymen as much as Christians all over the world.

$ 9,80

Softcover, 78 Pages

ISBN 978-1-533676-30-6